Queen of Puddings

5 oz breadcrumbs
1 tbsp vanilla sug
grated rind of 1 lemon }

Put into pudding basin.

1 pint milk }
2 oz butter }

Bring to just below boiling point & stir into c[...]

Leave for 10 mins & beat in 4 large

Pour mixture into greased shallow 2½ pint

Bake at 64 for 25 m[in]s.

Warm 2 tbsp blackcurrant or Rasber[...]
(if you use jam, sieve it) &
spread it over custard.

Whisk 4 large egg whites. Add 4 oz c[...]
Pile onto the pud. Sprinkle on 1 tsp su[...]
Return to oven for 15 mins.

hmmm...... it really is very sweet!

also, it seemed more exciting when I was a child,
simply because I didn't know how it was made
& couldn't imagine.

ORLANDO GOUGH
RECIPE JOURNAL

A CELEBRATION OF EXTRAORDINARY HOME COOKS, NO.2

A

PUBLICATION

First published in 2012
by TOAST
Matrix House
Swansea
SA6 8RE

Designed and typeset by TOAST
Printed in England by TJ International Ltd, Padstow, Cornwall

ISBN 978-0-9564115-1-8

www.toast.co.uk/publishing/orlandogough

To Jessi, the best home cook I know.

Introduction

Orlando Gough is the sort of cook who can, apparently effortlessly, produce a delicious three course meal for twelve people while all those people are in his kitchen, drinking copious wine and talking loudly. And he can do it while joining in the conversation. Cooking has become second nature to him and is inseparable, in his world, from a relaxed conviviality. It's cooking to nourish both body and soul.

He's also a cook of distinct character. His recipes might stem from Sussex or from the Levant but, knowing him as I do, I think I could recognise all of them as his. That's not, of course, that they taste the same as each other but that his cooking has its own handwriting: not fussy, not parading itself but wide ranging, heartwarming – and very tasty. He's the epitome of a good home cook and a man entirely at ease with himself in the kitchen.

Other than that? He's a remarkable composer, a great harnesser of the human voice in all its wonderful manifestations. He's clever – double first in maths from Oxford. He's the good parent, with his wife Jo, of Daniel and Milo – and here I suppose I must declare an interest: the four of them are among my favourite people in the world. I hope this doesn't throw into question all I've written above. It shouldn't – I've spent very many happy evenings in many different locations enjoying Orlando's meals. I'm very happy now to be able to provide the opportunity for you to enjoy them too.

James Seaton, Toast. 18.10.12.

Prologue

I grew up in a public school where my father was a teacher. Our flat had a roof terrace directly above the school kitchen, with a central section raised on a low wall, in which was a series of air vents. My brothers and I thought it was hilarious to stuff anything we could lay our hands on – earth, moss, chewing gum, whatever – through the vents, hoping that it would find its way into the school lunch. This was my first experience of cookery, or rather guerrilla cookery.

My mother very wisely taught us to cook when we were very young. She had taught herself when she got married during the war by copying out recipes from cookbooks in her local library in Louth, Lincolnshire. Some of these recipes survived in her personal cookbook – strange concoctions like Herrings in Claret. In 1950 Elizabeth David's *Mediterranean Cooking* came out and the cooking habits of my parents, like so many other middle-class people, were revolutionised. Rationing was still in force, and the ingredients were often difficult to find; but the exuberance of the recipes was inspiring.

Nevertheless, the first dishes I learnt to cook were deeply old-fashioned – Claggum (a kind of toffee – you needed a new set of teeth for every bite) and Rhubarb Crumble. They came from a book called *Farmhouse Fare*, which also included some bizarre and evocative wartime recipes like Mock Duck, a mixture of grated carrot and Bisto moulded into the shape of a duck.

Elizabeth David is still my favourite cookery writer. Compared to most modern recipe books her style was austere. She had no desire to be liked and was famously intolerant, not to say rude. (When Jancis Robinson, interviewing her on the television, asked her why she wrote *Mediterranean*

Cookery, was it because she wanted to change British cooking habits? etc. etc., she left a disorientating pause and replied – 'For money of course'.) But in fact she unquestionably did change British cooking habits with her unfussy versions of classic European recipes.

I started writing down recipes in a notebook when I was in my twenties, and I still have it and use it. It's chaotic and scruffy and some of the recipes are almost buried under a thin layer of the food they describe, but it's a treasure to me because it's a history of my family life, full of notes, comments and annotations ('fry the onions while trying to stop Daniel from screaming...'), as well as being a kind of culinary history of the last forty-odd years – for example there's a recipe for Stilton Soup which was flavour-of-the-month in about 1975, and one for John Dory with Candied Aubergines which seemed like a good idea in 1995 but which prompted me later to write, simply, 'per-lease'.

The recipes in this book are written purely for my own benefit, partly as a reminder and partly to make myself laugh. They're all pretty sketchy; some of them are just diagrams. So there was a bit of work to do to make them usable.

Orlando Gough. 06.09.12.

QUANTITIES

The recipes I've given here serve four generously (with the exceptions of the big celebratory meals, which serve more, and the Tortilla, which serves one).

ACCURACY

The apparent accuracy of the amounts and the cooking times makes them look non-negotiable. In fact they're extremely negotiable, and I encourage you to experiment. The only recipes which need a large degree of accuracy are those which involve baking – cakes, scones, soufflés, and oddly enough, the granola which needs pinpoint precision. I have to admit that '180°C' on our oven means 'slightly to the right of the splodge on the dial which might once have read 200°C'. Though it's worth saying that these recipes have been tested by someone who is not only a brilliant cook, but has a proper dial on her oven.

A PLEA FOR QUASI-AUTONOMOUS HOME COOKING

Should home cooking be significantly different from restaurant cooking? I think it should, not just on weekday evenings but generally. It makes obvious sense to avoid recipes which require several sous chefs, fridges full of stocks and sauces, ingredients which are impossible to find, kitchen equipment you'd need an extension to house, etc. That's not to say that complexity is out – it's immensely satisfying to make a complex dish successfully; but there are many recipes which work much better in the home than in the restaurant – a traditional Sunday lunch, a suet pudding, scones… And of course there are key differences socially – at home the cook is going to serve and eat the meal, so the structure of the meal needs to be looser, more informal.

QUALITY OF INGREDIENTS

I have tried not to insult your intelligence by specifying the quality of the ingredients. I have assumed that your food shopping is informed by a mixture of your interest in food, your conscience and your bank balance – so no need to talk about 'organic eggs' and 'extra-virgin olive oil'. By the way, how can something be extra-virgin? Surely virginity is strictly binary? And anyway, have you ever tried to buy olive oil that is simply virgin? Let's have a moratorium on ridiculously inflated language. And for that matter, what does organic mean? It seems to be a very slippery concept.

WHAT TEMPERATURE TO SERVE STUFF AT?

There are dishes which clearly benefit from being teleported from stove to table, such as pizza (in fact one of the drawbacks of pizza is that it's compromised by every second it spends on your plate – ditto fish and chips). But many dishes are better lukewarm – like the Blackberry Clafoutis on page 82 – or cold. For example, it's clear that the taste of cooked fruit becomes fuller as it cools, and I think, with absolutely no scientific justification, that the same is true for vegetables. So dishes like the Catalan Spinach and Broad Beans with Fennel and Mint on pages 75 and 77 are very good cold – not fridge cold, room-temperature cold. Of course texture matters too, and some dishes become claggy when they cool, but generally I think cold food is underrated.

ORDER

The recipes appear roughly in the order I learnt them, and therefore in the order they appear in my own recipe notebook. If you're looking for something specific there is an index at the back of this book which allows you to search for an appropriate dish in a number of different ways.

Contents

*

A comprehensive index of selected topics can be found at the back of this book.

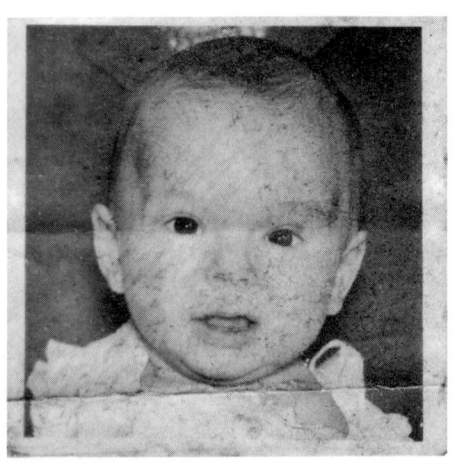

1950s

The end of rationing, Fanny Cradock,
a small patch of rhubarb, Brenda Lee,
Suez, short trousers, Diana (the magazine),
olive oil from Boots, the pressure cooker.

Rhubarb Crumble

–

At the age of five I had my first garden – or rather I had a small patch in my parents' garden – and I grew, exclusively, rhubarb, a clever choice of crop for a five-year-old, because it's practically indestructible. Looking back, I like the purity of this venture. It didn't make me into a gardener, but it did lead to a love of rhubarb crumble.

Ingredients—
750g rhubarb
100g caster sugar
the peel of an orange
200g plain flour
125g demerara sugar
125g butter
crème fraiche (to serve)

Method—
Heat the oven to 200°C. Chop up the rhubarb, put it in a saucepan, and add the sugar and orange peel. Add a few tablespoons of water, then simmer gently, uncovered, until the rhubarb is soft and has lost its shape. Important: there should be almost no liquid left. Taste it, and add more sugar if you like (but bear in mind it will have a very sweet topping, so it's better tart). Remove the orange peel, and pour into an ovenproof dish. Meanwhile put the flour and butter into a bowl. Rub the butter into the flour. Add the sugar. Pour this mixture over the rhubarb, and bake for 25 minutes. Serve with crème fraiche.

*

This dish is very good cold.

Baked Eggs

–

My parents often used to have these for lunch with homemade bread rolls. The eggs are not actually baked, and I think they should be called *Oeufs en Cocotte*, but the name has stuck in our family. There's a more elaborate version involving cream, but I prefer this ultra-simple one. It's very good with a little salad of broad beans, mint and Manchego cheese (though of course this rather compromises the beautiful economy of the original dish).

Ingredients—
4 eggs
butter
salt and pepper

Method—
Put four ramekin dishes into a frying pan. Pour cold water into the pan to half way up the sides. Into each ramekin put a little lump of butter and bring the water to the boil. When the butter is melted, break an egg into each dish, and season with salt and pepper. Put a lid on the pan and check after three minutes.

Daphne Gough's Cheese Tarts

–

My mother made these whenever my parents gave a drinks party.
This seemed to happen about twice a week – well maybe a bit less.
In summer the drink was usually white wine with peaches; in winter it
was often brandy and ginger ale – wonderfully consoling, in fact the
perfect drink for a wake. Then there was a (slightly punishing) New Year's
Day party at midday, where they served Irish Coffee. My father claimed it
was a perfect pick-me-up. I found it made me feel queasy, even if I'd had
a blameless night the night before.

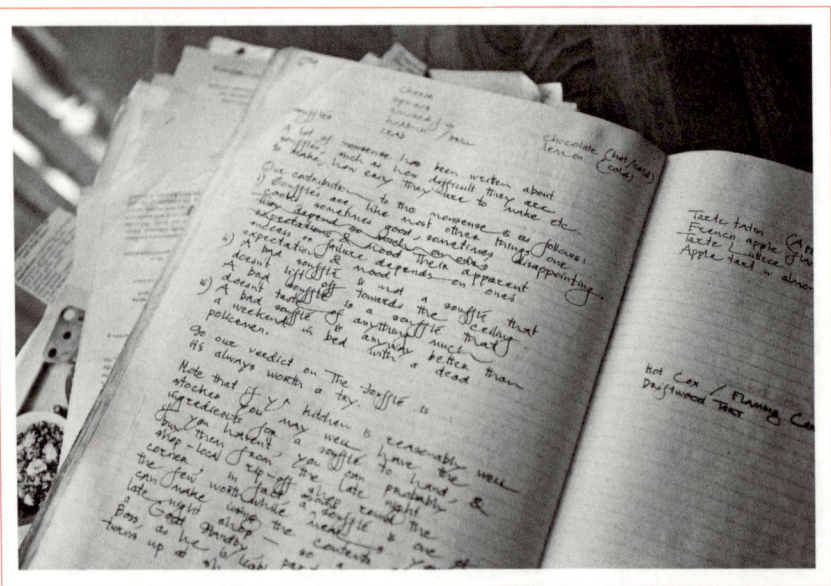

Ingredients—

200g plain flour

100g butter

1 egg yolk

3 eggs

160g strong cheddar cheese, grated

40g parmesan cheese, grated

6 tbsp double cream

generous pinch of cayenne pepper

salt and pepper

Method—

Heat the oven to 200°C.

Make the pastry by rubbing the butter into the flour with a generous pinch of salt (or whizzing them together in a blender); mix the egg yolk with a few tablespoonfuls of water and add. You may need a little more water to bring the pastry together.

Roll out the pastry, cut it into circles to fit the indentations in a tartlet tin. Butter each indentation, put in the pastry, prick a few holes in it and bake blind for 10 minutes.

Meanwhile beat the eggs, and mix in the grated cheeses, the cream and the cayenne pepper. Season to taste.

Take the pastry out of the oven, put a tablespoonful of the mixture into each tartlet, and bake for another 12 minutes. Serve hot. Preferably don't make them in advance.

Prawn Pilaff

—

My maternal grandmother lived next door to us for twenty years.
We played Canasta and Scrabble obsessively. She told me a story which
was part of the family mythology. She goes into a hat shop, and sees
two blue straw hats. They are identical except in one respect – one has
a beautiful garland of flowers round the brim. Actually two respects –
the plain one is more expensive. She asks why. The shop assistant says:
'Madam is paying for the restraint.'

This recipe is a good example of the restraint principle. It's ridiculously
simple, and delicious. The simplicity can feel like a lack of sophistication,
but I don't think it should. Maybe the real sophistication is in daring to
leave things out. I've tried cooking this more like a conventional pilaff,
with onion and spices, but somehow it's not as good.

If you can only get almonds with skins, pour boiling water over them,
leave them for five minutes, and squeeze them from the fatter end.
They should shoot out of their skins.

*

By the way, it must be basmati rice or it won't have the same subtlety of flavour.

Ingredients—

150g almonds, without skins

300g basmati rice

400g shelled king prawns

50g butter

salt and pepper

Method—

Roast the almonds in the oven at 190°C for 15 minutes till they're light brown. Check occasionally to make sure they don't burn – it can easily happen. Cook the rice in 600ml water – it'll take about 12 minutes. Drain and refresh with cold water. Melt the butter in a frying pan, add the prawns and cook gently for a couple of minutes. Add the rice; let it heat through for a couple of minutes, stirring in the prawns. Season with salt and pepper, and toss the almonds on top. Good with a green salad into which you've cut up a few slices of fried streaky bacon.

1960s

Indoor shoes, the Yardbirds, Kennedy,
Elizabeth David: *French Provincial Cooking,*
Zandra Rhodes, bacon and fried bread,
free love (but not for me), punting, log tables,
the Higgs Boson, the fondue set.

Mackerel (Four Ways)

(all recipes are for four mackerel)

–

My feelings about mackerel are bound up with my first experience of catching them – on Loch Hourne in Western Scotland where my brother Jamie and I went to stay with his schoolfriend Nicholas Scott. Jamie was twelve and I was eight, so it's very surprising that I was invited. The mackerel were dead easy to catch (though dead difficult to kill) and in the boat with us was a beautiful girl, tantalizingly older than me, on whom I had a glorious, agonizing crush, my first ever. I've never seen her since. When I mentioned this holiday to my brother recently, he remembered only how spooky and desolate the loch was, and he didn't even remember that I was there (upstart younger brothers!). He also revealed that he had a crush of his own – on Nicholas Scott.

So, given that the ideal way to experience catching and eating mackerel is to be out on a boat on a Scottish loch with a brazier and Teresa D'Abreu (or Nicholas Scott), and given that it's not always possible to organise...

TRY THEM GRILLED. Heat the grill to its maximum possible temperature. Make two slanting incisions in the flesh on each side of the gutted and cleaned fish, season, and grill them for 7 minutes on each side. Serve with a sprinkling of lemon juice, and perhaps a little **relish:** chop up 80g green olives finely, and add 3 tbsp chopped parsley, 2 tbsp capers and 3 tbsp raisins; mix in 1 tsp honey, 1 tbsp vinegar and 3 tbsp olive oil.

TRY THEM BAKED EN PAPILOTTE. Heat the oven to 190°C. Chop up a small bunch of parsley, and the fronds of two fennel bulbs (the rest of the fennel can be used to make an accompanying salad – see page 81). If you grow herb fennel, use a small handful of the fronds. Mix in 3 tbsp capers, the grated zest of a lemon, and a pinch of cayenne pepper. Season with salt and pepper.

Put a quarter of this mixture inside each mackerel. Butter four pieces of greaseproof paper generously and wrap a mackerel in each one. Put the parcels in a baking dish. Bake for 20 minutes.

TRY THEM BAKED WITH POTATOES. Slice 600g new potatoes thickly (three or four slices from each potato.) Parboil them for 12 minutes or so. Sprinkle a little olive oil over, put them in an ovenproof dish, and bake them in a 200°C oven for 15 minutes, till they are beginning to brown. Meanwhile prepare four mackerel. Make two slanting incisions in each side of the gutted and cleaned fish, put a little sliver of lemon in each incision, and season. Make 90g breadcrumbs by whizzing up day-old white bread in a food processor, and mix in the chopped leaves of a small bunch of parsley. Season the mixture. Slice up four cloves of garlic and fry them gently for a few minutes in 150ml olive oil, taking care not to burn them. Put the mackerel on top of the potatoes, sprinkle over the breadcrumb-parsley mixture, and finally sieve the frying oil over the top (discarding the garlic). Clap the dish back in the oven for 15 minutes.

TRY THEM COLD. Put the fish in a large frying pan. Add a couple of bay leaves, a few slices of lemon, white wine vinegar to taste, some peppercorns and a little salt. Cover with water, bring to the boil, put a lid on, and simmer very gently for 15 minutes. Leave to cool. Serve with a tarragon sauce (see page 81) or a **sauce remoulade:** hard-boil two eggs, peel and pound to a paste with a few drops of vinegar. Mix in an egg yolk (raw) and half a teaspoon of mustard, and then gradually add 125ml olive oil, beating all the time, as if you were making mayonnaise (which, essentially, you are). Stir in a tablespoon of white wine vinegar or more to sharpen the taste. Finish off with 1 tbsp of chopped tarragon and 2 tbsp chopped capers. If you can't find fresh tarragon, use two tablespoons of finely chopped small pickled gherkins (cornichons). Drain the mackerel before serving.

Slow Beef Stew

–

This is a classic old-school Provençal *daube*. Serve it with mash, or baked potatoes, or, best, a dish of buttery egg noodles. The pork rind isn't mandatory, but it does give the stew a gorgeous richness.

Ingredients—
2 onions, chopped
6 cloves of garlic, chopped
180g bacon, cut into thin strips
2 carrots, sliced
olive oil
1kg shin of beef, in slices
100g pork rind
3 tomatoes, peeled and chopped
the peel of half an orange
a large glass of red wine
bouquet of thyme with a couple of bay leaves
salt and pepper

Method—
Heat the oven to 150°C.
Fry the onions, garlic, bacon and carrots together in a casserole dish for 15 minutes. Add the beef, pork rind, tomatoes, orange peel, wine and bouquet of herbs, and bring to the boil. Season, and put in the oven for 2½ hours. If the stew starts to dry out, add more wine. Remove the pork rind and the bouquet of herbs at the end of the cooking. Just before it's ready, make a **persillade** by chopping together a small handful of parsley and 2 cloves of garlic. Serve separately. It should be sprinkled on top of each plate of stew.

*

*Alternatively, and equally good, at the last moment
add a generous handful of stoned black olives.*

Sussex Pond Pudding

–

At the age of seven I was bundled off to boarding school, to be greeted
by daily cold baths and dreadful food. We ate meals at four long wooden
tables, in the middle of one of which was a drawer. The person sitting
in front of this drawer had a very important job, which was to covertly
accept plates of inedible food, and empty them in. On most days the
drawer filled up – and was then mysteriously emptied by the kitchen staff.
Nothing was ever said: an example of the curious mixture of repressive
and laissez-faire tactics that boarding schools practised.

Not all the food was horrible. The suet puddings were excellent –
Dead Man's Leg, Spotted Dick, Chocolate Stodge... But they never
cooked my favourite suet pudding, the sublime Sussex Pond Pudding.
It's true to say that one doesn't exactly get thinner when eating
this pudding, but it's worth it.

Ingredients—

250g self-raising flour
125g shredded beef suet
75ml milk
75ml water
180g butter, cut into small chunks
180g caster sugar
1 large lemon, pricked deeply with a knife

Method—

Butter a 1½ litre pudding basin generously. Mix the flour and suet in a bowl. Make into a dough with the milk and water. Roll about three-quarters of the dough into a large circle to fit the bottom and sides of the pudding basin. Roll out the rest to make a lid.

Drop the large circle of pastry into the basin. Put half the butter and sugar in, then the lemon, then the rest of the butter and sugar. Place the pastry lid on top and press the edges together, if necessary using water to seal.

Put a piece of foil over the basin. Tie it in place with string. Put the basin into a saucepan big enough to allow the basin to be lifted out. Pour in boiling water to half way up the side of the basin, cover, and simmer for 3 hours, topping up with boiling water if necessary.

Take the saucepan off the hob, lift out the basin and take off the foil. Ease the pudding from the sides of the basin with a knife. Put a (not too shallow!) dish over the top and turn the whole thing upside down.

When you cut into the pudding there should be a gorgeous pond of buttery syrup. Cut the lemon into pieces – it'll be soft but still tart. Serve with cream.

Scones

–

These very rough scones were a family favourite when I was a child. We often ate them at Sunday breakfast, with homemade marmalade (see opposite). The point here is the lack of sugar, which makes perfect sense I think considering that they're always eaten with sweet stuff.

Ingredients—
300g self-raising flour
½ tsp salt
100g butter
about 150ml milk, preferably sour

Method—
Put the flour in a bowl with the salt. Add the butter and rub it in as if you were making pastry. Add enough milk to make a soft dough. Shape roughly into balls – about eight of them. Put them on a floured baking sheet and bake at 190°C for 15 minutes. You can add extra baking powder, but I'm not convinced it makes them any better.

Serve hot. My parents used to make them with no fat, which is fine but you have to eat them immediately.

Peter Gough's Marmalade

–

This is the marmalade my father used to make – chunky and bitter, the best I've tasted. It has less sugar than most marmalade recipes, so it needs to cook for longer. To make the best use of the pectin in the pips, they are left floating free during the cooking, and taken out at the end. Obsessive work, but worth it. Seville oranges, curiously, seem to be the last strictly seasonal fruit. So marmalade-making marks the passing of the years, giving it a rather beautiful significance.

Ingredients—
3kg Seville oranges, 6 litres water, 5kg sugar

Method—
Cut up the oranges into chunks – you choose the size. Put them in a large saucepan and pour in the water. Bring to the boil and simmer with the lid on till they're soft – at least two hours. Take the lid off, and add the sugar gradually, stirring all the time, keeping the mixture at a rolling boil. When the sugar is dissolved, keep the rolling boil going, and stir attentively rather than continuously. Eventually, after a further two hours or so, as the liquid becomes more dense, the pips will start rising to the surface. As they appear, remove them with a tablespoon. Test the marmalade in a cold saucer. It should pucker up when tilted. Most people sterilise their jam jars by putting them in a slow oven for half an hour. We never bother.

If the marmalade seems a bit thin, you can boil it up again. Or, when you're ready to eat a jarful, pour it in a bowl and leave it for a couple of days to thicken up. As a last resort, you could add pectin to thicken it. My father would turn in his grave.

Mum's Plum Cake

–

This is an old-school fruit cake. It's become a commonplace to express a preference for moist cakes. I can see why, but I've got a weak spot for this kind, which has a texture more like a rock cake. Back in the day people seem to have preferred drier cakes – for instance French Sand Cake (there's a recipe in Margaret Costa's excellent *Four Seasons Cookery Book*) which seems to suggest that sandiness was considered desirable in a cake. An extreme version of this thinking prevailed in the household of my uncle Tenniel when he was a child. His guardians (his aunt and uncle) wouldn't allow a cake to be eaten until it was several weeks old. This is clearly daft but I can almost see what they were thinking. This Mum's Plum is good cold; it's insanely good hot. If you find Christmas Cake hard-going, this is an excellent substitute.

Ingredients—
350g self-raising flour
500g dried fruit
1 tsp mixed spice
½ tsp grated nutmeg
180g caster sugar
½ tsp salt
3 beaten eggs
180g melted butter
1 tbsp black treacle

Method—
Butter a large cake tin, using greaseproof paper on the bottom. Mix all the ingredients in a bowl, adding a little milk if the mixture feels too stiff. Pour into the tin, and bake at 160°C. Test after 50 minutes. A skewer should come out clean – but only just. Leave in the tin for 15 minutes before turning out.

Lemonade
–

No-nonsense homemade lemonade – simple and excellent,
a domestic version of the wonderful *Citron Pressé*.

Ingredients—
3 lemons
3 tbsp caster sugar
1 litre cold water

Method—
Peel the zest from one of the lemons and put into a jug.
Squeeze the lemons and add to the jug.
Add the sugar, pour in the water and stir.
Taste for sweetness, adding more sugar if you like.
Leave for at least 15 minutes to steep.
Ice is of course a possibility, but not mandatory.

*

Good made with a mixture of lemons and limes.

1970s

Stilton soup, Frank Zappa,
MSG, the three-day week,
Margaret Costa: *The Four Seasons Cook Book*,
squatting, gulub jaman, Vivi Richards,
Malcolm McClaren, the chicken brick.

Corned Beef Hash

–

This is a seriously old-school dish. Corned beef, in a bizarre tin with its
own key, was a feature of 1950s cookery, but is now on the endangered
species list, along with spam, tapioca, condensed milk, tinned ravioli,
dried mixed herbs and various other items which will probably
not be much lamented.

Corned beef – a kind of salt-cured boiled beef – was invented as a means
of preserving the meat. Curiously the kind you can buy in tins seems to
have been minced. It's not great eaten straight, but it works surprisingly
well in this simple recipe. This dish is creeping back on to the menus of
groovy restaurants – quite rightly I think.

It was a staple dish of our household when I was squatting in Warren
Street, in North London. Its advantage, apart from being cheap, was that
it could be produced on our cooker, a one-ring Baby Belling. Because of an
idiosyncrasy of our electrical system it was only possible to use the ring or
the oven at any particular time, so the one-pot dish was king.

This shortcoming of the house, one of many (chronically leaky roof, rats,
lack of hot water etc. etc.) may have had some connection with the fact we
were informally supplying electricity to Boy George who lived next door,
a show of generosity I'm very proud of. Surely Karma Chameleon wouldn't
have been possible without this hijacking of the national grid?

Ingredients—
4–5 medium potatoes
1 large onion, chopped
2 cloves garlic, crushed
olive oil
340g tin of corned beef
salt and pepper
a couple of tablespoons of chopped parsley

Method—
Boil the potatoes. As they cook, fry the onion and garlic in olive oil till soft. Chop up the potatoes and add. Cook this mixture over a medium heat for about ten minutes, stirring frequently. The trick is to get the potatoes to brown while not burning the onions. Now add the corned beef and cook for another five minutes. The corned beef will lose its rather brutal look and become amalgamated with the onions and potatoes. Season with salt and pepper, toss over the parsley and serve. If you have enough rings on your cooker, boiled cabbage is the ideal accompaniment (preferably Savoy).

P.S. 'Round the corner from our squat was Drummond Street, where the first Southern Indian restaurants in the UK were opening, including the wonderful, indestructible Diwan-I-Am. So our diet ricocheted between dhosas and corned beef hash – an early example of extreme multiculturalism.

Cumberland Sauce

–

Cold gammon (page 79) served with baked potatoes, green salad and
Cumberland sauce – the ideal Boxing Day meal. Best not to do the
usual sugar glaze with the gammon, good though it is – the whole thing
becomes too sweet.

Ingredients—
4 tbsp redcurrant jelly (about 375g)
6 tbsp port
large pinch of ground ginger
2 tsp Dijon mustard
salt and pepper
the peeled zest of an orange

Method—
Melt the redcurrant jelly in a saucepan. Add the port and ginger, and
barely simmer for ten minutes. Put the mustard in a bowl and add some
of the sauce gradually, stirring all the time. Pour this mixture back into
the saucepan and cook for another couple of minutes. Allow to cool.
Season with salt and pepper.

Meanwhile slice the orange zest crosswise into very thin strips. Put in
a saucepan, cover with water, bring to the boil, poach for three or four
minutes. The idea is to take some of the bitterness out of the zest – but
not all, because it helps to mitigate the sweetness of the sauce. Drain,
refresh with cold water, and add to the sauce.

*

This sauce keeps well in the fridge for at least two weeks.

Chicken and Merguez Couscous
(serves 8)

–

In the mid-1970s the Oxford Boat Race crew had been beaten by Cambridge several years running, and the coach, Dan Topolski, decided to change the system. In the two week run-up to the race the crew, instead of staying in a stultifying West London hotel, would live in a rented house, with a cook. On the basis of a brilliant meal at a dinner party, he asked my brother Piers, an architect, to cook for them. Piers rowed me in, along with my then-girlfriend Celia, equally unqualified (though she has since become a brilliant professional cook, so we should probably have left the whole thing to her).

What do you cook for beefcake in training? In defiance of tradition, not to say common sense, we cooked what we normally cooked. The naivety of it is breath-taking. Nowadays the crew probably has an army of nutritionists alongside the sports psychologists, physiotherapists, shamans and brand awareness managers. But, coincidence or not, the crew started winning... and went on winning for years and years.

It was tempting to serve endless steaks because the crew had sponsorship from Dewhursts the butchers – ethically a rather dubious deal as the managing director Lord Vestey was being investigated for tax fraud. But we didn't, and Piers in particular re-educated the rowers' tastes. He was also very good at renaming classic dishes for the occasion: Treacle Tart became Driftwood Tart, Baked Bananas became Hot Cox.

We cooked this couscous, or something like it, for them. This is a great dish to make for an occasion. It's frisky, it's sociable, it's delicious. In the original Moroccan version, the meat – lamb usually – is boiled with the vegetables. This version is filtered through Paris and Spitalfields Market, where there was a brilliant couscous café that was unfortunately obliterated in the recent yuppification of the market. This dish takes some effort to prepare, but is worth it.

You can substitute the Merguez with other spicy sausages, but it's a pity, because merguez have a very distinctive taste – for one thing they're made with lamb. Like most stews this is almost better the next day, so you could make it in advance.

Ingredients—
1.2 kg boneless chicken, a mixture of breast and thigh
a small bunch of tarragon, chopped
a large lemon
olive oil
salt and pepper
16 Merguez sausages
2 large onions, chopped
5 cloves garlic, crushed
8 tomatoes, skinned and sliced
a generous pinch of saffron – about 50 threads
50g ginger root, peeled and chopped
1 tsp cinnamon
300g carrots, thickly sliced
300g turnips, peeled and cut into eighths
300g frozen broad beans (or 500g fresh broad beans)
300g courgettes, thickly sliced
500g chickpeas, cooked
a bunch of parsley, chopped
a bunch of coriander, chopped
750g couscous
harissa (see overleaf)

Method—

Cut the chicken into chunks and put in a bowl. Mix in the chopped tarragon, the juice of the lemon, a few tablespoons of olive oil and season with salt and pepper. Marinate for a couple of hours at least. Make into eight kebabs.

In a large saucepan, fry the onions and garlic in olive oil for ten minutes. Add the tomatoes, saffron, ginger, cinnamon, carrots and turnips. Cover with water or stock, bring to the boil, cover the pan, and simmer for twenty minutes. Add the broad beans, courgettes and chickpeas and simmer for another five minutes, until all the vegetables are done.

There should be plenty of juice, so if it's getting too dry, add some extra liquid. Finally season with salt and pepper, and stir in the parsley and coriander.

Meanwhile barbecue (or grill) the kebabs and the sausages. Give the kebabs six minutes on one side, turn them over and give them another six minutes; that should be enough, but check by opening up one of the chunks. Be careful not to overcook them – they'll get very dry.

In the old days couscous was cooked in a special couscousier, steamed above the stew. Nowadays it's pre-cooked; all you have to do is to put it in a bowl, mix in a few tablespoonfuls of olive oil and pour over a litre of boiling water. Give it a stir and leave it for a few minutes until the water is absorbed. Break up any lumps with a fork.

Serve with harissa. You can buy readymade versions, but they tend to be a bit generic, and it's easy to make at home (see opposite). Serve half the harissa straight, and half mixed with a few ladlefuls of the liquid from the stew.

*

This recipe works well with fish kebabs instead of meat. A vegetarian version, missing out the meat entirely (and using vegetable stock obviously), is also very good.

Harissa
–

Ingredients—
50g fresh, hot red chillies
2 cloves garlic
1 tsp ground coriander seeds
3 tsp caraway seeds
1 tsp cumin seeds
1 tsp salt
5 tsp olive oil

Method—
Deseed the chillies, and then whizz together all the ingredients in a blender.

A Lamb Barbecue

(serves 8)

—

When I was young our standard family holiday was to take two camping punts from Oxford to Lechlade and back on the River Thames, a style of holiday that has gone seriously out of fashion, but which gave me a taste for both punting and wood-fire barbecuing. I find barbecuing with charcoal dull in comparison, so at home we have a large fire bowl and use wood. I love obsessing over the fire and trying to control the heat by moving the wood around, keeping a jug of water at hand to douse any flames. I must be a man.

MY FAVOURITE MEAT FOR A BARBECUE IS A BUTTERFLIED LEG OF LAMB. I've always thought that marinades were fairly pointless for barbecued meat, as the flavour from the wood smoke is so good, so I usually just season it before cooking (though barding it with rosemary and anchovies is always good). It takes about 35 minutes to cook. When it's cooked, put it on a heated serving plate, leave for a few minutes, so that some of the juices come out, and squeeze over a couple of lemons before carving it.

TO ACCOMPANY, BARBECUED POTATOES: wrap medium-sized potatoes carefully in foil and bury them in the embers at the same time as you begin to cook the meat – only possible if you're using wood.

SERVE WITH A CHICORY SALAD.

Ingredients—

4 heads chicory

20ml white wine vinegar

120ml olive oil

1 tsp mustard

at least 8 chopped anchovy fillets

at least 1 tbsp small capers

3 tbsp chopped parsley

Method—

Divide up the chicory and put in a bowl. Make a dressing with the vinegar, oil, mustard, anchovies and capers. Mix it with the chicory. Sprinkle over the parsley.

(If you're not making the barbecued potatoes, roughly chop up ten cooked new potatoes and add them to the salad.)

ALTERNATIVELY, BUY 5 TINS OF COOKED FLAGEOLET BEANS, AND ROAST THEM in a 200°C oven for 30 minutes with at least 6 cloves of chopped garlic, salt, pepper and a few tablespoonfuls of olive oil. The beans should end up with a crunchy crust. Dead easy and really good. If you like, stir in the chopped flesh of a large peeled tomato before cooking. Serve with a green salad.

Apricot Nut Bread
–

This arrived in our family via the magazine *Vogue*. In principle a fashion magazine is unlikely to be a good source of recipes, but this loaf, halfway between cake and bread, is delicious. Butter is essential. The loaf is very dense, so it should be cut as thin as possible. Butter the cut face before slicing.

Ingredients—
250g dried apricots
30g butter
½ tsp salt
180g caster sugar
1 beaten egg
100g wholemeal flour
375g plain flour
1 tsp baking powder
125g walnuts, quartered
1 tbsp sugar
1 tbsp milk

Method—
Slice the apricots thickly. Put them in a large bowl with the butter, salt and sugar. Pour over boiling water to cover. Leave for 10 minutes. Add the egg, then the flours and the baking powder, and finally the walnuts, mixing each in well as you go. Pour into a buttered bread tin and bake at 180°C. Test after 50 minutes. A skewer should come out clean.

As soon as you take the bread from the oven, paint over a glaze made with 1 tbsp sugar dissolved in 1 tbsp milk. Leave to cool.

Summer 1986

1980s

The miners' strike, John Adams,
Thatcher (but not for me), Kate Bush,
the Hacienda Club, the cappuccino,
Diana (the princess),
Claudia Roden: *A New Book of Middle Eastern Food,*
the wok.

Tomato and Anchovy Tart

—

This is a version of the lovely Provençal dish *anchoïade*, which is
made with bread dough, much like a pizza. I usually make it with pastry
because I never remember to start cooking supper until it's too late
to make yeast dough. So what kind of pastry?

I've made puff pastry only once in my life, for the 25th birthday dinner
of my wife Joanna. It was soon after I'd met her and I was keen to impress…
It was a hot day in August, and I failed to keep the pastry cool. It gradually
turned into a shambolic sticky mass which I threw out of her kitchen
window in a rage. It landed on the wall at the far end of the back garden
(I am a keen cricketer), where it stayed for weeks, because the garden was
an almost impenetrable jungle of stinging nettles. The pastry gradually
melted down the wall like a Salvador Dali painting, a continuing reminder
of my over-ambition and bad temper. It's a great tribute to Jo that she
forgave me for buggering up her birthday dinner. But I'm very happy
making shortcrust pastry. I don't really like bought pastry, but if you do,
you can make this recipe with bought puff or shortcrust.

Ingredients—
200g plain flour
100g butter
salt (for the pastry) & pepper (to season)
1 egg yolk
500g good small tomatoes, such as cherry plum, halved
3 cloves garlic, chopped
olive oil
at least 6 tinned anchovies, cut in half lengthways
at least 10 black olives
a small handful of basil

Method—
Heat the oven to 200°C.

Make the pastry by rubbing the butter into the flour with a generous pinch of salt (or whizzing them together in a blender); mix the egg yolk with a few tablespoonfuls of water and add. You may need a little more water, but be careful not to let the mixture get too soggy. You want it to be a dry as is possible to roll out without it breaking up. If you let the dough rest in the fridge for 30 minutes it will be easier to work with.

Butter a large tart tin or baking sheet. (This tart doesn't need sides.) Roll out the pastry, put it on the sheet, prick a few holes with a fork, and bake it blind for 15 minutes.

Meanwhile, fry the tomatoes and garlic for three minutes in olive oil. Season. Drain the mixture so that there's almost no juice. You can use the juice instead of olive oil to make a salad dressing – delicious.

Take the pastry from the oven. Put the anchovy halves on top, pour over the drained tomato mixture, and clap it back into the oven for ten minutes (whoops, beginning to sound like Jamie Oliver... put it back in the oven). While it's cooking, pit the olives and cut them in half, and tear the basil leaves in pieces. As soon as it comes out, spread them both over and serve.

Our friend Andrew who, despite being a photographer rather than a musician, taught me more or less all I know about world music, makes a wonderful tomato tart quite similar to this; but instead of baking the pastry blind, he puts a very thin layer of mustard on to protect it from the juice of the tomatoes and bakes them both together.

Mushroom Filo Pie

–

This is a version of the Greek *tiropita*. It's good for lunch or a light supper.
And an opportunity to plug my favourite Greek restaurant, the wonderful
Lemonia in Regent's Park Road, London, where I first ate *tiropita*.
The freshness and simplicity of this kind of Greek cooking is a delight;
it's cheap, and it's a great place to meet up with David Temple, director
of the wonderful Crouch End Festival Chorus.

Ingredients—

400g mushrooms
3 cloves garlic, crushed
olive oil
400g feta cheese
a small bunch of coriander, chopped
pepper
8 sheets filo pastry
100g butter, melted
sesame seeds (optional)

Method—

The trick is to buy (or of course forage for) mushrooms which actually
taste of something – not that easy to do. Oyster mushrooms work well.
Slice them up and fry them with the garlic in olive oil for a few minutes,
until they've softened up. Crumble the feta into a bowl, and mix in the
mushrooms and coriander. Add pepper (hold the salt – feta is very salty).

Butter a baking tray, lay out a sheet of filo, brush melted butter on to it,
lay out another sheet on top, and so on. After four sheets, spread over the
mushroom and cheese mixture, then continue to lay out filo sheets and

brush butter. Attach sheet 4 to sheet 5 by dabbing water round the edge and pressing together. Brush the top sheet of filo with butter, sprinkle on some sesame seeds if you like, and bake at 190°C for 25 minutes.

Fish Stew

(serves 8)

–

Making authentic *bouillabaisse* (the Mediterranean fish stew) in Britain
is tricky because we don't have the right fish. Elizabeth David says,
basically, don't bother – and then gives three mouth-watering recipes.

So this is a riff on *bouillabaisse*, *bourride* and various other Mediterranean
fish stews, with the distinctly un-Mediterranean addition of smoked fish.
I think the idea came from a stonking magazine part-work of the 1980s,
called *Good Cooking on a Budget*. Really? What budget?

The recipe looks insanely laborious, but it's not. All in all it takes about
75 minutes to make. To make a very frisky version, add in some seafood
when you're cooking the fish at the end – shelled prawns, squid, mussels.
Don't use shell-on prawns as the spiny bits come off and get stuck
in your teeth.

FIRST MAKE A FISH STOCK. This isn't essential (you can use water)
but it does significantly improve the final taste. If you buy fish from
a fishmonger, they'll give you some bones and trimmings. At the
supermarket, they probably won't have a clue what you're talking about.

Ingredients—
Fish bones and trimmings
1 onion
1 carrot
2 bay leaves
150ml white wine

Method—

Put all the ingredients into a saucepan with 3 litres of water.
Simmer for half an hour. Strain.

MEANWHILE MAKE AN AIOLI.

Ingredients—

2 egg yolks
1 tsp mustard
125ml olive oil
125ml sunflower oil
6 cloves garlic, peeled

Method—

Put the egg yolks and the mustard in a bowl. Mix together the oils and
gradually beat them in, starting with a few drops at first and then adding
more a bit at a time, making a mayonnaise. (The mustard makes this
process much less fraught.) Crush the garlic and add to the mayonnaise.

If you prefer the garlic in your aioli less bitter, parboil the garlic cloves in
water for three minutes. Pound to a paste and add to the mayonnaise.

NEXT MAKE A ROUILLE.

Ingredients—

2 thick slices of white bread
3 red chillies
3 cloves garlic, peeled
5 tbsp olive oil

Method—

Soak the bread in a little fish stock for a minute or two.
Put all the ingredients into a blender and whizz them up.

NOW THE STEW ITSELF.

Ingredients—

1 large onion, chopped

1 large head fennel, chopped

olive oil

600g ripe tomatoes, skinned and chopped

750g potatoes, cut into chunks

400g carrots, sliced

3 litres stock or water

300g French beans, trimmed and cut in half

a generous pinch of saffron – about 50 threads

1 kg white fish fillets (haddock, grey mullet, hake all possible, even oily fish such as mackerel)

500g smoked fish fillets (haddock, cod)

200–400g raw seafood such as shelled prawns, bearded mussels, squid rings (optional)

salt and pepper

a generous handful of parsley, chopped

lots of French bread, sliced

Method—

Fry the onion and the fennel gently in the oil for at least 15 minutes till soft. Add the tomatoes, potatoes, carrots and stock (see recipe on previous page) or water. Bring to the boil and simmer for about 15 minutes, till the vegetables are nearly cooked. Add the French beans and the saffron, and cook until the beans are only just tender. Then add the fish and seafood, and cook for another three minutes or until they're cooked through. Adjust the seasoning and sprinkle on the parsley.

In the final stages of cooking the stew, dry out the bread for a few minutes in a 180°C oven, or toast it lightly.

Serve the stew in wide soup bowls, as deep as possible. Each person spreads some rouille on a slice of bread and puts it into the stew. Serve the aioli separately. Dollop it on, but don't stir it into the stew.

Eat with a spoon.

Spiced Pork, Beetroot and Polenta
(serves 8)

—

This is another big celebratory dish, a strange hybrid of Chinese and Italian cookery, absolutely delicious. I can't remember where it came from, so apologies to anyone who should be given the credit.

Double the amount of polenta you make (see overleaf) to serve 8 people. It's easiest to buy cooked beetroot, but is best to cook them yourself.

Ingredients—
a loin of pork, boned and rolled, weighing about 2kg, the skin separate
2 tbsp coriander seeds
2 tbsp sesame seeds
4 tbsp white wine vinegar
6 tbsp oil
6 tbsp honey
6 tbsp soy sauce
2 tsp Dijon mustard
2 cloves garlic, crushed
12 medium-sized beetroot
50g butter
salt and pepper
3 tbsp coriander leaves, roughly chopped

Method—

Crush the coriander seeds in a mortar and pestle or by rolling them with a rolling pin. Put the sesame seeds in a frying pan over a medium heat for a few minutes until they go light brown.

Put the vinegar, oil, honey and soy sauce in a saucepan over a low heat till the honey dissolves and the mixture amalgamates. Put the mustard, coriander seeds, sesame seeds and garlic in a bowl, and stir in the hot mixture. Allow to cool for a few minutes, and then use the mixture to marinate the meat for a few hours.

Wrap each beetroot in silver foil and bake them at 180°C for what seems an insanely long time – at least two hours. In the same oven and for the same length of time, roast the meat in its marinade. If the juices threaten to dry up, add some water.

For the last 40 minutes, put the skin, salted and oiled, on a separate tray in the oven to make crackling. You may need to turn up the heat at the end of cooking (while the pork is resting) to give the crackling a good colour.

At the end of cooking, let the pork roast rest. Unwrap the beetroot, let it cool for a few minutes, and then grate it coarsely. Add the butter, season with salt and pepper and serve alongside the pork.

The marinade becomes the gravy; the fat will need to be drained off as much as possible. Toss the coriander leaves over the meat before carving. Serve with a green vegetable and the polenta.

If there's some pork left over, eat it cold with a fennel salad (see page 81).

Polenta

–

Usually polenta is cooked in water. I'm not normally in favour of faffing around with well-conceived simple recipes, but I think this really is an improvement on the plain version. The polenta to use is the type that has been partially pre-cooked (actually it's quite difficult to buy polenta which hasn't).

Ingredients—
600ml milk
an onion, cut into quarters
a bay leaf
5 tbsp polenta
20g butter
40g grated Parmesan
½ tsp Dijon mustard
salt and pepper

Method—
Put the milk in a saucepan with the onion and the bay leaf. Bring slowly to just below boiling point, turn off the heat and leave for at least half an hour so that the flavours of the onion and bay leaf infuse the milk.

Take out the onion and bay leaf. Bring the milk back to just below boiling point, and add the polenta, stirring all the time. Cook for five minutes over a low heat, stirring, if not continuously then watchfully. The resulting mixture should be slightly liquid. Add the butter, the parmesan and the mustard, and season with salt and pepper.

This is also delicious served with grilled Italian sausages and red onion marmalade (see opposite).

Red Onion Marmalade

–

I remember red onion marmalade as being a product of the Cuisine Minceur movement of the 1980s. Can this be true? It contains an awful lot of sugar... This is excellent served cold with patés and terrines. Hot with sausages and mash it is a staple of our family diet. I particularly like mash made with half potatoes and half celeriac. Champ is also very good – just add some chopped spring onions to the mash.

Ingredients—
4 medium red onions, sliced not diced
olive oil
4 tbsp demerara sugar
4 tbsp white wine vinegar

Method—
Fry the onions gently in oil till soft. Add the sugar and vinegar, and cook, uncovered, over a very low heat for an hour, stirring from time to time to prevent sticking. The marmalade should be thick and gooey with just a hint of liquid left.

Chocolate Soufflé

–

This soufflé comes from before the era of the ubiquitous death-by-chocolate pudding – of which I must own up to being a fan. This is less extreme, so there's a danger that it might now seem namby-pamby, but I think it's very good.

Will it rise? Will it fall? Don't worry. What's really important is not to overcook it, otherwise it's death-by-chocolate-but-not-in-a-good-way. Adding 2 tbsp brandy to the mixture enhances the taste but slightly compromises the texture, I think.

Ingredients—

180g plain chocolate

4 egg yolks

2 tbsp caster sugar, flavoured with vanilla if possible

6 egg whites

Method—

Butter a soufflé dish.

Melt the chocolate. (The simplest way is to break it into a bowl, and pour boiling water over. Leave for a couple of minutes, make sure it's soft, and then pour off the water. Weird, but it works.)

While the chocolate is melting beat the yolks vigorously with the sugar until they are almost white. Add the melted chocolate. In a separate bowl, beat the egg whites till stiff, and fold into the chocolate mixture. Pour into the soufflé dish and bake at 190°C for 18 minutes, no longer. The inside should be slightly runny. Serve with cream.

Almost better than this is an **apricot soufflé:** made with 125g dried apricots. Put them in a baking dish with 50g caster sugar, cover with water, and put in a 180°C oven for 40–50 minutes. (Alternatively you can cook the apricots on top of the stove but it seems to me this results in a less intense apricot flavour.) Drain and liquidise. Add 2 tbsp brandy and the grated rind of half an orange. Mix in 4 egg yolks. Fold in 6 well-beaten egg whites. Pour into a buttered soufflé dish, and bake at 190°C for 20 minutes.
Serve with cream.

I made this successfully with prunes instead of apricots recently.

1990s

Rose Gray and Ruth Rogers: *River Café Cook Book*,
lemon grass, sixteen kinds of tomatoes, Black Wednesday,
Pulp, raves, Pokemon, Edwina Currie, salmonella,
BSE, the pasta-making machine.

Pan Bagnat

–

An absolutely brilliant Provençal sandwich. I first had one at a party in Laughton Tower, a folly in the middle of a field near Lewes in Sussex, where our friends Charles and Romilly made about a thousand of them for the occasion. I thought it was the best cold picnic food I'd ever had. It's like *Salade Niçoise* in a bun. I am normally an evangelist for the single-ingredient sandwich, but this is the honourable exception.
I haven't specified the amounts – improvise.

Ingredients—
a flatish loaf of good bread, such as ciabatta
a selection of: anchovy fillets, sliced tomatoes, strips of red pepper, broad beans, stoned black olives, capers (but not tuna)
pepper
olive oil

Method—
If the broad beans are young, use them raw. If they're not, cook them first and let them cool off. Put the loaf on a board and cut it in half horizontally. Cover one half with a mixture from the list above, season with pepper (hold the salt), drizzle over some olive oil, and put the top half of the loaf back on. Put another board on top and something heavy on top of that. Leave for at least half an hour.

Cullen Skink

—

This is a lovely comforting Scottish smoked fish soup. It's like a
thin chowder. After some very enjoyable holidays in rural Scotland,
slightly compromised by the quality of the food, my wife Joanna and
I had an embryonic plan to open a restaurant in the delightful town of
Newton Stewart in Galloway, where we were going to serve Cullen Skink
and haggis. Partly out of laziness, and partly due to a realisation that it
was an eye-wateringly patronising idea, this never happened.

Ingredients—
125g smoked bacon
1 tbsp butter
1 large onion, chopped
4 medium potatoes, thickly sliced
stock or water to cover
450g smoked haddock
350ml milk
salt and pepper
a small bunch (but not too small) of parsley, chopped

Method—
Cut the bacon into strips. Fry it gently in a large saucepan till the fat runs
out. Add the butter and the onion. Fry for 10 minutes till the onion is soft.
Add the potatoes, cover with water or stock. Simmer for 15 minutes.
Meanwhile, poach the haddock in the milk for 15 minutes. Flake the
haddock. Keep the milk! Add the haddock and the milk to the other pot,
and cook everything together for a couple of minutes. Add salt and pepper
and chopped parsley.

Risi e Bisi

–

This is my fall-back risotto.

I used to put chopped mint into this dish – a modern addition. Is it
any better? I'm not at all sure, and I think that we often over-elaborate
traditional dishes. Of course we need to look at new ways of interpreting
them, but there's a danger that adding more ingredients masks the ones that
are there. And I think there's a problem of reaching for the mint every time
we cook peas – it's a good relationship but can't they play away occasionally?

Ingredients—

1 medium onion

olive oil

300g Arborio rice

1 glass of white wine

1½ litres stock (chicken or vegetable)

200g shelled peas (I own up to using frozen ones)

90g Parmesan cheese, grated

a knob of butter

salt and pepper

Method—

Fry the onion gently in the oil for 10 minutes or so till soft. Don't let
it brown. Mix in the rice, and add the wine and the stock. Let it barely
simmer, uncovered, for about 20 minutes, until the rice is *al dente.*
It should be more liquid than a normal risotto, a small step on the way
to being a soup, so if necessary add more stock or water.

About five minutes before the end, cook the peas separately. When the rice
is done, stir in the peas, the cheese and the butter. Season. Cover and leave
for five minutes, Serve with more grated Parmesan if you like.

Corsican Seafood Pasta

–

This is an attempt to recreate a wonderful dish we had at a beach restaurant near Ile Rousse, in Corsica – a dangerous enterprise, the success of which can't now be tested, because the restaurant has changed hands. Do you have to be on a beach in Corsica to achieve full enjoyment of this dish? Possibly, but seems to taste good in Brighton too.

I have to admit to having made this dish, not just once but several times, with a couple of natty little packets of mixed cooked seafood on special offer at a well-known supermarket. The Corsicans would have screamed in horror, but we liked it.

Ingredients—
1 onion, chopped
olive oil
8 tomatoes, skinned and chopped
5 cloves garlic, crushed
salt and pepper
a glass of white wine
20 threads saffron
a mixture of seafood – say 200g squid, 200g shelled king prawns, and 400g mussels (and indeed anything else that you fancy, such as langoustines, alternatively ring up Rick Stein, make your apologies, and use 500g mixed cooked seafood)
100ml double cream
500g spaghetti
a small bunch of parsley, chopped

Method—

To skin the tomatoes, pour boiling water over them and leave for five minutes. If the skins don't come off easily then buy riper tomatoes next time.

Prepare the squid: pull out the quill, remove the guts, peel back and remove the skin, and cut into rings. Clean and de-beard the mussels, throwing away any open ones.

In a thick saucepan, fry the onion in olive oil till soft. Add the tomatoes, garlic, salt and pepper. Cook gently for a few minutes. Then add the wine and saffron, cover the pan, and simmer for 30 minutes. Cook the spaghetti in plenty of boiling water till al dente (about 10 minutes). Drain.

Meanwhile, steam the mussels in a small amount of water till they open (about three minutes), fry the squid and the prawns for a couple of minutes.

At the last moment, stir the cream into the tomato sauce.

Add the squid and the prawns, and mix it all into the spaghetti.

Put the drained mussels on top, and sprinkle over the parsley.

Chicken Polo
(serves 4–6)

–

This wonderful dish originates in Iran – it's not all mad mullahs
and political posturing there.

We served it at my fortieth birthday party at which forty people
somehow managed to eat a meal in the main room of a small terraced
house in North London. If you wanted to leave the room for any reason,
you had to be passed over the tables by the other guests.

Rice cooked in this way is utterly delicious in itself.

Ingredients—

8 chicken thighs

olive oil

1 large onion, chopped

300g basmati rice

75g butter

125g dried apricots, each one sliced in three

the crushed seeds from 8 cardamom pods

40g raisins

1 tsp ground cinnamon

200ml chicken stock

salt and pepper

Method—

Using a large frying pan, brown the chicken thighs in a few tablespoons of olive oil. Add the chopped onion and fry gently for 15 minutes.

While the onion is frying, boil the rice for 10 minutes in 600ml water (rule of thumb: twice the weight of the rice). Rinse it very thoroughly under the cold tap to get rid of the starch. Melt the butter in a thick-bottomed saucepan, add the rice and a little salt, and stir. Put on the lid of the saucepan, wrapped in a tea towel, and cook over a very low heat for 45 minutes. A crunchy light brown crust, known in Iran as dig, should form on the bottom of the rice.

Once you've got the rice on, add the apricots, cardamom seeds, cinnamon, raisins and chicken stock to the chicken and onions. Season. Empty the mixture into a saucepan, cover, and simmer over a low heat for 45 minutes, making sure it doesn't dry out. You should be left with a few tablespoons of luscious sauce.

Empty the rice onto a dish, break up the crust, and mix in the chicken stew.

2000s

Choirs, sexing up the dossier,
star anise, credit default swaps,
egg and bacon ice cream, climate change,
Sam and Sam Clark: *The Moro Cookbook*,
the death of the turkey twizzler, the tagine.

A Tortilla that would surprise a Spaniard
–

When I'm by myself I often make this tortilla. I've never actually cooked it for anyone else, so it's a bit strange to be putting it in a book. The recipe serves one (for obvious reasons).

Ingredients—
1 large potato
1 clove garlic, chopped
3 small or 2 large eggs
salt and pepper
olive oil
1 tbsp chopped parsley

Method—
Chop the potato into tiny cubes, about the size of a pea (but cubic obviously). Using a small non-stick frying pan, fry the potatoes in a few tablespoons of oil over a medium heat, turning frequently, for about 8 minutes, till they are browned and cooked through. Add the garlic about two minutes before the end – it's important not to burn it.

Beat the eggs, season, and pour them over the potatoes. Lower the heat, and cook for a few minutes until the egg is more or less cooked through. Sprinkle over the parsley, fold the tortilla over and serve.

If you prefer to cook the egg completely, turn the tortilla over: slide it on to a plate, put the frying pan upside-down on top of the plate, and invert (good luck). Cook for another few minutes.

Catalan Spinach

–

This recipe works well with fried courgettes instead of the spinach. At my fiftieth birthday party, our friend India, who was about twenty-one, fried enough courgettes for 150 people while dealing with a cannonade of mobile phone calls and explaining to me the incredibly subtle and Machievellian techniques by which she dealt with boyfriends. It was an awe-inspiring feat of multi-tasking.

Like a lot of vegetable dishes, this and the courgette version are surprisingly good cold. They can be eaten as a room-temperature starter, as part of a buffet, or as a cold accompaniment to a main course.

Ingredients—
500g spinach, washed
2 cloves garlic, chopped
30g pine nuts
50g raisins
olive oil
salt and pepper

Method—
Cook the spinach in the water which clings to the leaves after washing until just wilted. Drain it obsessively by squeezing out the water with your hands.

Meanwhile heat three tablespoonfuls of olive oil in a frying pan. Add the garlic, pine nuts and raisins. Cook for a two minutes over a medium heat. The raisins should be slightly caramelized and some of the pine nuts browned. Put the spinach in a bowl, season, and pour the nut and raisin mixture on top.

Black Pudding Accompaniments
–

I love black pudding – the British type (the best versions of which are from Bury and Stornaway) the French *boudin noir*, the Spanish *morcilla* – all of them insults to vegetarians, and all absolutely delicious. My son Milo and I have a weakness for a weekend total fry-up which has to include black pudding.

It's dead easy to cook – it just needs to be sliced and fried in a little oil for a minute or two on either side. *Morcilla* needs care – it tends to break up easily (which by the way makes it a very useful ingredient for enriching stews).

Here are two good accompaniments:

CARAMELIZED APPLES
Ingredients—
50g butter (clarified butter or ghee are better, actually)
3 Cox's apples, cored and sliced but left unpeeled
2 tbsp chopped parsley

Method—
Melt the butter over a medium heat, being careful not to burn it. Put in the apples and cook gently till golden brown on one side. Turn them over and brown the other side. The apples should be soft but not mushy. Sprinkle over the parsley. You can add a splash of cider, but I prefer the plain version.

BROAD BEANS WITH FENNEL AND MINT

Ingredients—

2 cloves garlic, chopped

½ tsp fennel seeds

olive oil

500g broad beans

100ml chicken stock

5 or 6 sprigs of mint, chopped

Method—

Fry the garlic and fennel seeds for a minute in a few tablespoons of olive oil. Add the broad beans and the stock, and cook for about 4 minutes, till the beans are tender. Stir in the mint, and season.

*

A good accompaniment to British black pudding is a potato hash *– make it exactly as for corned beef hash (see page 34), but leave out the corned beef.*

A way with Lentils
–

How come lentils have such a bad reputation? It's bizarre. Did they appear in one too many dreary Zen Stews? It wasn't their fault.

I discovered Puy lentils via the excellent Cod with Lentils and Salsa Verde from Simon Hopkinson's brilliant *Roast Chicken and Other Stories*.
This was the beginning of the *Salsa Verde* era. It's a great sauce, though it has a tendency to blow away some of the things it's paired with
(come to think of it, that's not its fault...)

The cooking time for the lentils is very critical – if you undercook them it's like eating shot, overcooked they become mushy and lose their astonishingly beautiful colour. They should be slightly *al dente*.
20 minutes is about right, but start testing after 15.

Ingredients—
250g puy lentils
a medium onion, chopped
1 carrot, finely diced
3 cloves garlic, crushed
olive oil
grated zest of half a lemon
salt and pepper

Method—
Fry the onion, the carrot and the garlic gently in olive oil for 20 minutes.
Meanwhile cook the lentils in plenty of water. Drain them. Add the onion and carrot mixture and the lemon zest, season with salt and pepper, and stir together.

Hot, these lentils are wonderful with boiled gammon – no need to be clever with the gammon. Just simmer it in water for an hour per kilo. Add a few tablespoonfuls of the broth to the lentils – and mustard sauce (see below)

Cold, they make a lovely salad. Just mix in a lemony dressing: (the juice of a lemon, half a teaspoon of mustard, a few tablespoonfuls of olive oil). Particularly good served with smoked fish and horseradish sauce, and an excellent component of a cold summer lunch (see overleaf).

Mustard Sauce
–

This is a simplified version of the classic French *Sauce Bretonne.* It's an interesting hollandaise–mayonnaise hybrid.

Ingredients—
3 egg yolks
3 tsp Dijon mustard
3 tsp white wine vinegar
2 tbsp chopped parsley
75g melted butter

Method—
Mix together the egg yolks, mustard, vinegar and chopped parsley.
Add the melted butter gradually, as if you were making mayonnaise.
It will be slightly thinner than mayonnaise – about the consistency of custard.

As well as being very good with boiled gammon and lentils (see above and opposite), this sauce is a lovely accompaniment to baked herrings.

A Summer Lunch

(serves 6)

–

This lunch, or something like it, we first had at the house of our friend Sarah who is an excellent cook despite the fact that she never seems to eat anything.

It consists of a cold roast chicken, accompanied by some but perhaps not all of these simple cold vegetable dishes:

LENTIL SALAD (essential) – see page 78.

POTATO SALAD (essential)

Cook 750g new potatoes, let them cool, and slice them up. Add 2 teaspoons of capers and 2 tablespoons of chopped chives. Make a **thin mayonnaise** with an egg (not just an egg yolk), a teaspoon of mustard and 125ml oil, mix everything together. Correct the seasoning.

TOMATO SALAD

Slice up 600g tomatoes (or use cherry tomatoes cut in half), pour over some olive oil, season (use lots of pepper), and, crucially, grate the zest of a lemon over.

GREEN BEANS AND HAZELNUTS

Make a **dressing:** with the juice of a lemon, a chopped clove of garlic, a teaspoon of mustard and a few tablespoons of olive oil. Peel the zest from half an orange, slice it crossways into very thin strips, and blanch them for 3 minutes in boiling water, drain. Roast 50g skinned hazelnuts for 15 minutes, cut them in half (sounds impossible but isn't!). Cook 600g beans for five minutes and drain with cold water immediately. Mix the dressing and the orange zest into the beans while they're still warm. Stir in the hazelnuts just before serving so they keep their crunch.

FENNEL SALAD

Slice a couple of fennel bulbs very thinly, add a ton of chopped parsley and a **lemony dressing:** combine the juice of half a lemon, half a teaspoon of mustard and a few tablespoonfuls of olive oil. Leave for at least half an hour.

TARRAGON SAUCE

You could, though it's by no means essential, serve the chicken with a tarragon sauce, basically a *salsa verde* but made with tarragon instead of basil:

a small bunch of tarragon (watch out, tarragon is very pungent)
a medium bunch of parsley
1 tsp Dijon mustard
1–2 tsp capers
3–5 anchovy fillets
½–1 tbsp white wine vinegar
100ml olive oil

Take the herbs off their stalks. Whiz up the parsley in a food processor with the oil and half of the rest of the ingredients. Taste and add the remaining quantities of the ingredients little by little. The sauce should be aromatic but not too sharp and the tarragon shouldn't overwhelm everything else.

Blackberry Clafoutis

–

There was a (minor) furore in the press recently about the denuding of the countryside by the middle-classes with their new interest in foraging. Damn – foraging always seemed to me not only innocent but inherently democratic, not to say a free-for-all. I must confess, I haven't stopped picking blackberries.

For a few years we actually had them in our garden. We lived in a beautiful house in a village in Sussex. Our benevolent landlord Denis had made his considerable fortune from care homes, and spent it mostly on a portfolio of random motor vehicles. He memorably drove into the middle of my fiftieth birthday party on a huge Harley Davidson with tassles, making a complete mess of his own lawn. One corner of the garden had been colonized by blackberry bushes. When my mother died, I abandoned work for three weeks and dug a vegetable garden. The brambles were extremely difficult to get rid of, and were always itching to reappear through the runner beans. In the six-odd years that have passed since we left, the house has been empty, and the garden is again full of brambles and Denis's clapped-out caravans. A surreal elegy to the passing of time.

You could argue that blackberries should only be eaten raw, preferably straight off the bush, but this version of clafoutis (normally made with black cherries) works well I think.

Ingredients—

500g blackberries
2 eggs
60g plain flour
pinch of salt
60g caster sugar
400ml milk, warmed
75g butter

Method—

Heat the oven to 220°C.

Beat the eggs, mix in the flour, salt and sugar. Add the milk gradually, stirring hard all the time.

Generously butter a tart tin (not one with a removable base). Put in the blackberries, and pour the batter over them. Dot with the rest of the butter, and bake until the top is set but not too firm. Check after 25 minutes.

Don't serve it hot, don't serve it cold, serve it lukewarm. Before serving you can sprinkle over some more caster sugar and, if you like, some rum.

Hazelnut Cake

–

This is a version of a lovely cake that my mother used to make, *Pain de Gênes*, using roasted hazelnuts instead of almonds. It makes a very good pudding, particularly if served with some kind of cooked fruit, for instance the Plums with Star Anise (page 88). It's also a good picnic cake. (I think one can argue that a picnic without a cake is not a picnic.)

Ingredients—
200g hazelnuts, without skins
200g butter, softened
200g caster sugar
5 beaten eggs
75g plain flour
1 tsp baking powder

Method—
Butter a large cake tin. Use a conventional cake tin with greaseproof paper on the bottom, or one of those ones with a central funnel. Roast the hazelnuts at 160°C till they're light brown – about 15 minutes. Let them cool for a few minutes, then grind them roughly in a blender. Cream the butter and the sugar, and beat in the eggs one at a time. Mix in the hazelnuts, flour and baking powder, and pour into the tin. Bake at 160°C. Test after 35 minutes. A skewer should come out clean.

Chocolate and hazelnut cake: try adding in 200g melted plain chocolate. You get a really lovely cake which people tend to mistake for brownies.

*

If you'd like a gluten-free cake, use polenta flour.

2010s

Milo tries to get a job in Nandos,
phone hacking, the Higgs Boson (again), Wikileaks,
superfoods, superinjunctions, cyclists in Lycra,
Fifty Shades of Grey.

Plums with Star Anise

–

We in Britain are periodically introduced to a new ingredient, partly due to global trade, partly to our comparatively generous attitude to immigration. This usually seems to result in a period of temporary overuse – think of the pesto pandemic of 2008, and look at the number of recipes in this book containing capers. After absorbing the traditional uses of these ingredients, we can begin to dream up hybrid dishes – sometimes inspired, like kedgeree, sometimes daft, like Peking Duck Pizza (yes, really).

Star anise, an ingredient in the marvellous Chinese five-spice powder, seems to go well with cooked fruit. This dish is good warm but best cold. Crème fraîche is a good accompaniment.

Ingredients—
8 plums, halved and stoned
80g caster sugar
1 wine glass marsala
5 star anise
1 vanilla pod

Method—
It's best if the plums are ripe, but you can make this dish with unripe plums (in which case allow extra oven time).

Put the plums in a baking dish, sprinkle over the sugar, and pour over the marsala. Split the vanilla pod in half and add. Dot the star anise around, and bake, uncovered, at 160°C for 45 minutes or until soft.

This recipe works well with apricots, peaches and nectarines too.

Julian's Granola

–

This recipe came to me recently from our friend Julian, music business lawyer and excellent cook. He had it from the proprietor of a delicatessen who told Julian he was leaving out one ingredient, presumably to ensure that Julian didn't immediately set up a rival business – which of course was his wicked plan. What that ingredient was I have no idea – the recipe seems to me brilliant as it is.

The quantities I have given make only about 10 servings, so if there are a lot of people in the house, you can find yourself chained to the stove. Try making larger quantities – you need to lower the oven temperature slightly, cook for longer, and turn over the granola several times during cooking.

You can of course vary the dry ingredients. I sometimes add a few hazelnuts, and, at the end, some dried cranberries. Julian uses sour cherries instead of raisins, but then he has a more lucrative job than me.

Ingredients—
60ml water
60ml sunflower oil
90ml honey
30g muscavado sugar
generous ½ tsp ground cinnamon
ungenerous ½ tsp salt
225g oats
75g whole skin-on almonds
60g sunflower seeds
60g pumpkin seeds
60g raisins

Method—
Heat the oven to 160°C.

Put the water, oil, honey, sugar, cinnamon and salt in a small saucepan
and heat it until the sugar dissolves.

Measure out the oats, almonds and seeds into the largest possible baking
tray. Mix in the syrup thoroughly. Spread out the mixture evenly.

Bake for 25 minutes altogether. Half way through, take the granola out
of the oven, break up any lumps and mix it around. The cooking time is
a delicate matter. If you overcook the granola, it becomes rather gritty.
Until you're confident, keep checking it as it cooks. It should go a very
light brown colour.

When the granola comes out of the oven, thoroughly mix it again,
adding the raisins. Store in an airtight container.

Galician Soup

–

A stonkingly nutritious Spanish soup that is nearly a stew. On a recent trip
to Madrid I realised that this dish could be seen as a coward's version of the
traditional *Pote Gallego*, which contains approximately these ingredients
along with about nineteen different kinds of meat, some of them very
mysterious. I'm a committed meat-eater, but I prefer this version.

Ingredients—
1 large onion, chopped
5 cloves garlic, crushed
olive oil
4 medium potatoes, in quarters
2 carrots, sliced
3 turnips, in quarters
½ Savoy cabbage, sliced thin
1¼ litres chicken or vegetable stock
20 threads saffron
2 tins cannellini beans (or use dried ones and cook them first heroically)
salt and pepper
250g chorizo (the soft, cooking type)
a small bunch parsley, chopped

Method—
Fry the onion and garlic gently in the oil for at least 10 minutes till soft.
Add the vegetables. Pour over the stock and add the saffron. Simmer for
15 minutes till the vegetables are cooked. Add the cannellini beans and
season. Simmer everything together for a few minutes. Meanwhile slice
the chorizo and fry it briefly in a hot frying pan with a small amount of
oil until it has coloured and the fat has exuded. Add to the pot, along with
the fat, and mix in the chopped parsley. Eat.

Index by Selected Topics

Tomato Salad   80

Gough

malade

oranges   (buy 10 lb — might have to
buy some away)   make sure they're
x sugar   really soft
pints water
t up the oranges & boil till soft.   2 hrs approx
water to make up ~~top~~ ~~~~~~ 18 pints — really!
g to the boil & simmer — rolling boil....
d sugar gradually.
mer... rolling boil   ~~REALLY DON~~
mer....
mer......   Turn down heat.
ing all the time. Remove pips as they come to the
in a cold saucer.   surface.

pots in the oven.
marmalade in pots.

y contentious step! In ordinary recipes you
t top it up. P. once told me to top it
to 27 pints — the resulting marmalade
more like a drink than a preserve.
pints seems about right...

3:5:6
oranges sugar pints of
  lb   lb   water
(by weight)